Her Name
is Mystery

A COLLECTION OF SPIRITUAL POETRY

Her Name *is* Mystery

RICHARD H. BARRY

To request permissions, contact the publisher at
hernameismystery@gmail.com.

Hardcover: 979-8-9877572-1-5
Paperback: 979-8-9877572-0-8
Ebook: 979-8-9877572-2-2

Library of Congress Control Number: 2023902765

First edition March 2023.

Edited by Malia Mendez
Cover and layout by Natalie Lauren Design

Excerpts from: "My Sweet, Crushed Angel," "Laughing at
The Word Two," and "Never Say It Is Not God" by Daniel Ladinsky,
© Daniel Ladinsky and used with permission.
www.danielladinsky.com.

Published by Richard H. Barry
hernameismystery@gmail.com

To Mystery and Her one-track mind.

To Hafiz, my soul's best friend, and to Daniel,
for making our friendship possible.

To Mike, who, once upon a time,
encouraged me to come out of the closet as a mystic.
Let's call this my coming out.

And to Jean, *amma*, who, when I felt as though
I was standing precariously on a ledge,
etched these tender words into my soul.

May you be at ease, even at home,
In your metamorphosing in the Kingdom among us.
And when your spirit is ready
And the timing seems good to you and the Spirit,
May you stand at the edge,
And leap,
And soar,
Leaving a trail of Light
For others to follow.

These poems belong to You, Jean, as much as they do to Me,
for it was your acceptance and validation that gave my spirit
permission to write them.

May they become that "trail of Light" you envisioned, one in
which at least a few others may bask.
Perhaps even follow.

Contents

Prologue: The Lot of Mystics

It's always the lot of mystics
To firmly be put in their place.

On the dunce's stool
By theologians,

In the bedroom
By God.

She Who Owns My Heart

Beyond knowing,
beyond experiencing,
beyond feeling,
beyond capturing,
beyond articulating,
her name is Mystery,
she Who owns my heart.

Known in unknowing,
experienced in intuition,
felt in unspeakable longing,
everywhere present, yet magically elusive—
oh, how she dances!—
articulated in groans and breathless hopes,
manifest ethereally in Love,
her name is Mystery,
she Who owns my heart.

I see her everywhere,
yet I cannot discern her.
I have unknown her always,
she Who cannot be proven,
she Who may not exist,
only because existence is an abode ill-suited to her,
a container not expansive enough,
a category not strong enough to hold her.

She is a black hole,
a gravity wave, ripping through space-time.
She is Dark Energy—
I have seen her,
but she danced away again.
How is it that she is so hidden and so present at once?—
oh, how she dances!—
Her name is Mystery,
she Who owns my heart.

She whispers the words "Higgs boson"
and dances away again.
Her retreating shadow is perceived in neuroscience,
as she vanishes in a pirouette.
She spins her way through quantum entanglement,
playfully mocking that cosmic speed limit,
for she is something more than light,
though light, too, hopes for her,
daring to hint at her Name.
Her enchanting laugh is in it all!

(Or am I hearing an echo of that laugh? I can't tell.
But what does it matter? It's enchanting either way.)

She is a quadrillion supernovae,
issuing forth countless,
imperceptible,
unnamed elements,
forcing the very boundaries of our universe to expand.
It is a timeless arabesque!

Oh, how she dances!

I have always loved her,
though I knew not her name,
though I was taught to call her by another,
a name which I have shouted for forty years.
But now I whisper her true name,
for she has made it known in my unraveling,
in my liquefying,
in my being unmade.
Her name is Mystery,
she Who owns my heart.

But as for *Homo sapiens*,
we who are gods,
yet whose eyes are only now beginning to crack open,
that we might take in our first glimpse
of the wondrous absurdity of life,
now these three remain:
presence, attention, and listening.
But the greatest of these are all three.
For these also are her names,
she Who owns my heart.

Why Not?

Why so many words?
Why so hurried?
Why not breathe?
Why not taste?
Why not notice?

Behold!
Each moment is bursting at the seams with the inexplicable.
How wondrously, how transcendentally ridiculous:
the fact that we *are*!
Absurdity and coherence in playful collusion,
their strange, melodious laughs synchronized,
in Holy Union,
indecipherable, one from the other,
and mischievously,
flirtatiously inviting us,
into each new miraculous nanosecond.
What unexpected bedfellows they are!

Why so many words?
Why so hurried?
Why not breathe?
Why not taste?
Why not notice?

The Grand Silence

This begins the Grand Silence,
in which we breathe,
and taste,
and notice.
But should Laughter break the Silence,
that is no sin,
for God is many things,
and laughter is his most enchanting form.

Idolatry

To call Mystery the "Trinity" is idolatry,
the type which She adores.
For each and every time we explain Her,
we commit idolatry again,
and there She is,
by our side,
no, in us,
sipping Her cup of aromatic tea,
giggling with pleasure,
committing idolatry in concert with us,
as She deigns to be known by names not Her own,
names which hardly suit Her,
but to which She graciously responds,
"Yes, and amen."

Taste

It started with the eggplant Parmesan.
I noticed it for the first time,
as if the ignition switch on my taste buds
had finally been activated.
"Oh, that's what a tomato tastes like,"
"Oh, that's the flavor of cheese,"
"Who knew a crouton could explode
like that when bitten into?"
Each bite a universe to be explored.
How am I only noticing this for the first time?
It makes me realize how often I have gluttonized on food,
but how infrequently I have enjoyed it.
Food has flavor, it turns out,
and I repent for how I have treated Her,
for how I have ignored Her.
Speaking of flavor,
(I feel silly even asking this, but...)
Have you met Sister Water?
Did you know that She, too, has a flavor?
And did you know that it is Sweet and Good?
She too is Mystery, she Who owns my heart.
For four decades I have not noticed,
I have not tasted.
What an adventure awaits!
To start anew and meet Her again,
one bite at a time,
one uncharted universe at a time.
Anchors aweigh,
the Journey begins!

Clearing Plots

It is said of some, few as they may be,
that they live in a different zip code.
Well, I have met more than two or three,
who have sauntered down those same roads.
They, too, have set up shop in that fairy-tale land,
and I see them clearing new plots,
but they seem so painfully unhurried!
It grates against my shortcut-addicted soul,
the leisurely pace they set,
but from a distance, I see them,
gathered around a freshly painted welcome sign,
attached to a newly cleared plot of land.
One repeats, in a gentle tone, "Rest, rest,"
Do I detect a South African accent?
One towers ten feet tall and intimidates me
with his deep voice and commanding presence,
even as I see him notice me, flash me a smile,
and clearly wave me over.
One cracks a joke he just couldn't hold back,
and everyone laughs disarmingly.
And four women, hand-in-hand,
are singing and dancing in a circle,
inviting me into Mystery.
And as I approach,
they step aside with a gleam in their eyes,
revealing the freshly painted sign.
And it's my name written upon it.
Hallelujah, they've cleared the plot for me!

Not Done With You Yet

"Come, let's argue this out," says the LORD.
Isaiah 1:18

Taking a few deep breaths,
I compose myself,
and turn to face the Divine:
"Excuse me, God, I have something to say,
a bone to pick with you, to be more precise.
There is too much inequity in this world,
too much harm, tragedy, and meaningless suffering,
too much naked exposure to absurdity,
for humanity to hold its tongue ad infinitum.
I stand as its representative today,
giving voice to our rightful grievances.
And I'll stop you before you even think of saying,
'Who are you to ask?'
What a cop-out!
Don't try to do to me what you did to Job.
No, you must answer to me.
Where are you when we need you most?
And don't tell me, 'The devil is responsible,'
when you've claimed to have defeated him.
Don't you dare try to shift the blame.
Man up!
I don't let my children get away with moves that cheap,
and I certainly won't let you either.
Nor tell me, 'He went through pain too.'
I didn't ask if you have felt our pains.
I asked why you didn't intervene
when the child was raped for the 500th time,
not to mention the 499 before.

I never claimed to be active in all things—
that was you.
I never claimed to be sovereign over all things—
also you.
I never claimed to be the Good Shepherd—
you did.
I never claimed to be the Defender of the Weak—
another one of your gems.
Let's riff here for a moment, shall we,
you who claim to defend the weak?
It's a strange title for someone who has such an extremely,
embarrassingly bad track record.
You seem great at defending well-to-do American evangelicals,
especially if they are white.
But you seem quite inept at defending the vulnerable.
Quite inept at safeguarding black men from systemic injustice.
Quite inept at saving child-trafficking victims,
or those of incest,
or three-year-olds who fall to malaria,
or countless women abused by arbitrarily powerful men.
How long is your arm, exactly?
It troubles me that it was long enough
to give us that special parking spot in Cabo,
but too short to reach them.
Keep your parking spots, and do your job,
oh, Defender of the Weak!
Or were you just embellishing on your resume?
If you could have stopped it, but didn't,
you are nothing short of a monster.
And if you intervene in any situation,
you're on the hook for it all.
So I will not answer to you,
You will answer to me.

'Where were you when I laid the foundations of the world?'
I've been told you are prone to ask.
What does that have to do with anything?
Stop trying to change the subject.
Stop trying to deflect,
you who refuse to be put on trial.
You can escape no more.
I don't accept your cop-outs,
your grandiose, condescending, entirely unbecoming excuses.
(Are you preparing to stand up?
No, stay right there, I'm not done with you yet!)
Another says, 'When you see God,
you will either shut up or fall on your face.'
I am still standing, my face uncovered,
meeting your gaze in defiance.
My heels are dug in, I'm not going anywhere,
and I'm not shutting up.
You *will* answer to me.
Let us return to your phrasing:
'Where were you when I laid the foundations of the world?'
Allow me to return the favor, though I'm not asking for your permission:
Where were you when the child was molested?
Where were you when the woman was abused?
Where were you when the HIV+ blood transfusion took place?
Where were you when the slave was lynched?
Where were you when the car-bomb exploded?
Were you busy arranging a pleasantly unexpected 25% discount on
Chanel handbags for all those pitiable, exhausted holiday shoppers at
South Coast Plaza?
#blessed
Were you otherwise occupied showering the privileged with trifles,
that the rich might more fully comprehend your favor upon them?
#grateful

Words are not failing me,
nor do I feel the slightest inclination to fall on my face.
You are on trial, not me, and your excuses are exposed at last.
You can no longer bully us.
You can no longer command us to ignore half of reality while crying
'Hosanna.'
'Holy, holy, holy,' you have demanded that we say.
No, I will stand my ground where Job wilted and lost his nerve.
I will teach my brothers and sisters to sing a new, fitting refrain:
'Horror, Horror, Horror.'
You've got some explaining to do.
What do you have to say for yourself?"

Then God,
in a movement both decisive and unhurried,
leans forward,
revealing an unexpected twinkle in his eye,
betraying the pleasure he took
in each and every word of my irreverent rant.
Slowly rising to his feet,
filling canyons with thunderous laudation,
he unreservedly gushes:
"Bravo! Bravo!
Well played, my dear!
I was swept up by your performance,
repeatedly forcing myself to restrain my applause,
for fear that I might miss a single word
or delightful turn of phrase,
not to mention you didn't seem too keen
on my attempted standing ovation earlier.
I love it when you get worked up like this,
your sass and your spunk reflecting my own!

It makes me wonder:
Might you be starting to grasp
just how much fun I find you to be?
And now, by way of response,
allow me to repeat the cliché:
'I don't believe in that God either.'
All those 'explanations,'
mere type and shadow, at best,
most just downright misleading and misled.
I'm sorry you've been forced to endure
the decodings of men,
as though tragedy were something to be deciphered,
rather than held in stunned, sacred silence.
I take no offense,
for those 'explanations' were not 'of Me,'
and I'm not very good at taking offense anyway.
I was too busy weeping to offer an explanation in the first place.
Rest, my sweet, crushed angel.
There is no explanation with which to contend today,
no argument to retort,
no accusation either.
I happily concede victory to you,
my stalwart little one,
for it is my joy to be overcome,
and your war was never with me to begin with,
but with well-meaning, though toxic, misconceptions.
You have fought a good fight,
and I am so very proud of you.
You have performed splendidly, my dear,
daring to defy your Beloved.
And don't be so hard on yourself as we waltz,
for as a dance-partner,
I am notoriously difficult to follow.

So let's sit one out for now.
Just know that I agree.
And you can rest."[1]

I should've seen them coming a mile away,
but his words still somehow take me off guard,
that inexpressible way he has about himself leaving me breathless.
Standing on wobbly legs,
undone in ecstasy,
I try to play it cool,
delivering my response with a well-understood wink,
"Rest? But I'm not done with you yet."

Just Beneath the Surface

Just beneath the surface,
scarcely concealed,
perpetually on the verge of bursting forth,
there exists a Smoldering Exuberance,
teeming joyously,
hoping to catch your eye, little one.
It is on pins and needles,
anticipating the pause you will one day take,
from your over-anxious struggles,
when your glance will finally happen upon It.
And in that moment,
your countenance will once again shine,
matching Its own,
your ears tingling,
and your soul instantaneously resurrecting,
at the sound of Its once obscured,
now irresistible invitation:
"Come and play!"

Unobtrusive

Like breath,
Filling, sustaining, mediating energy and vitality,
Without so much as announcing its presence,
Or publicizing its effects.

Like a mother,
Meeting countless needs,
Without keeping record of services rendered,
Or even hinting at a need for compensation.

Like a baritone,
Whose harmonies blend so well as to go undetected,
Yet without which something feels strangely amiss and incomplete,
Adeptly relating to notes both above and below.

You do not jockey for position,
Nor do You self-promote,
There doesn't seem to be a braggadocious bone in Your body.

So, please, My Dear, tell me Your dazzling secret:

How is it that
Every
Single
Thing
Is shot through with You,
Yet You remain
So
Very
Unobtrusive?

This Silly Little Game

We can see You, You know?
Like a skyscraper crouching to hide
behind a pebble,
or an elephant standing on its hind legs,
sucking in its gut,
in a comically failed attempt
to match the slender frame of a light post:
You aren't really cut out for
this silly little game we play.
And even if we couldn't see You so easily,
Your constant, barely restrained giggling
would give You away every time.

But since You seem to be having so much fun,
we will close our eyes
and count to ten once more,
for it must be admitted:
Your attempts at concealing Yourself
are entirely adorable.

We can see You, You know?
But why should we stop playing,
when our sides are splitting with Laughter,
at this silly little game we play?

Be Careful!

It's a startling phenomenon:
If you don't pay attention,
You'll never so much as notice It.
But be careful!
If you do pay attention,
You'll never notice anything else.

Facade

Keeping up the facade
Of separation from God
Is the hardest work
You will ever do

Try as you may
To make it look easy or natural
Your efforts will inevitably come off
As forced and contrived

And if you so much as pause
Or take in a full breath
Or let your guard down for the blink of an eye
It will all come flash-flooding back

The levees will be breached
The jig will be up
The charade exposed
The theatrics revealed as mere playacting

So resist if you must
And erect your imaginary walls of delineation as it suits you
For awaiting the collapse of Her beloved's ramparts
Is one of Mystery's most refined specialties

I wish you good luck
And you're going to need it
If you are to persevere
For even one more day

For keeping up the facade
Of separation from God
Is the hardest work
You will ever do

Serious Business

I caught Mystery in the act,
Red-handed, as it were,
Having ten times more fun,
Than my weary, beleaguered soul could have ever deemed appropriate.

But to my great astonishment,
As I was nobly taking offense on behalf of all humankind,
She didn't seem to be troubled in the least,
By my so clearly having spotted Her scandalous behavior.

And would you believe it?
She had the gall, the audacity even,
To waltz right up to me,
Feigning nonchalance as She whistled an obviously made-up tune.

And with an uninvited, flirtatious look in Her eye,
She brushed away an imaginary speck of dust from my shoulder,
Then darted away mirthfully,
Chanting, "Tag, you're it!"

Why, I didn't ask to be flirted with!
Or included in Her untimely antics!
How wildly inconsiderate!
Doesn't She know what serious business I'm always up to?

And here I now lie,
Melted into a puddle of rapture by Her touch,
Trapped in the loop of Her impish song and dance,
Unable to so much as attend to all my oh-so-serious business!

Smile

How else shall I put it?
The universe, existence, whatever "this" is:
It all adds up to
One
Big
Questionably Appropriate
Undeniably Marvelous
SMILE

This May Sound Familiar

[1]Salvation has never been very much about a legal transaction whereby your sins would be absolved in a heavenly court of law; it has always been much more about you dying to an old way of life, dominated by self-interest, and living out a new way of life, marked by other-inclusive, self-giving love. It has always been about your "false self" losing more and more of its control and your "true self" increasingly taking the reins — a type of death and resurrection, sound familiar? So if you truly desire this type of salvation, a type that demands inexpressibly more of you than the transactional model, though is no less dependent on grace, then stay on course in learning to live it out.

[2]Set your intention and strengthen your resolve to nurture your true self, while compassionately reminding your false self that he is no longer needed. Become committed to living a life of self-giving love, of finding your good in the good of others, of listening more to your prefrontal cortex than to your amygdala.

[3]Regard the life ruled by self-interest as having died in you, and marvel at how the farcical barriers between your life and God's are vanishing before your very eyes, even as you feel yourself "coming home," that is, being dissolved into the life of God; and that in some mysterious sense, you always have been.

[4]And some day, when Love has finally won out, when Its ways rule on earth "as they do in heaven," you'll be right there, celebrating and included in the victory.

[5]Want to put things in starker terms? Why not perform a public execution of your old way of life — that way in which you pried your own private good from the close-fisted grips of others,

convinced, as you were, that recognition, honor, purpose, meaning, validation, money, and even love, were all ze-ro-sum games?

⁶It's this impoverished mindset that has sent so many on a downward spiral of self-and-other-destruction, giving us the glimpses of hell on earth we see today, and insidiously wet-nursing those we fear to be looming just over the horizon.

⁷Of these bitter truths you are well-aware. You've "been there, done that," and you're fed up with self-interest's rule.

⁸That's why you set off on this new path to begin with, because every time you wres-tled the fruit of self-interest from the bloodied, scram-bling pile, successfully ex-tracting and consuming your sordid meal-for-one, you were left hungrier than when you started. It simply wasn't working!

⁹So let's not pretend like it ever did. Rather, how about we take our old, ill-fitting rags of privatized self-interest, toss them in a pile, and light 'em on fire?

¹⁰Who needs 'em any-way, when the garments of self-giving love look so damn good on us? It's as if we were made for these Royal Gowns!

¹¹Take a look around: Have you ever seen such a hand-some bunch? Now keep look-ing: in this divine attire, can you even tell who's who any-more, or where one ends and another begins? As we give ourselves in love to one an-other, doesn't everyone and everything seem to breath-takingly, inexorably melt into God? In the end, what is there to see besides Him!?!

¹²And as long as you've been given access to Mys-tery's wardrobe, I want you to go all out. Try on all of Love's accessories! Put on that crown of compassion. Don those bracelets of kind-ness. Sport that blazer of community. Flex those cuf-flinks of creativity. And get comfy in the plush robe of gentleness — gentleness not only toward others, but also

toward yourself, dear one.

[13]You and God both know what a miraculously tangled web of conflicting impulses your brain represents. So as you're in process of carving out new neural pathways, of learning to preference neo-cortically-informed thinking and behavior, be as tender with yourself and others as you've always known the Spirit's caress to be.

[14]And above all, remind yourself often that God, from whom existence flows and in whom the dance itself takes place, is Love. Pay close attention to my choice of words. I didn't say God is a person who is really loving, a concept we can wrap our minds around well enough. I said God *is* Love, a mind-bender that should keep us up at night, even as we blissfully lose ourselves in its embrace.

[15]May the peace of self-forgetfulness be yours, now and always. And may you be swept up by wonder, by awe — living in a state of perpetual amazement, that is, living spiritually.

[16]Soak in Holy Scripture; seek out and apply the wisdom of those who've made "the journey" before you; and make use of every means at your disposal to express your heart to God. Write a poem, sing a song, drop a beat, dance your heart out, propose a toast. Get creative in your celebration of Love!

[17]Do it all — and I mean absolutely everything — in Love's indescribably precious name, which is to say, of course, in the name of the Most High God. And I'll go first: you'll find this letter embossed with Love's seal.

To Hitch

I'd like to take this moment,
to publicly thank Mystery,
for the ministries of pastors
Hitchens,
Dawkins,
and Harris.
Where has this poet seen God in recent years?
In the Divine, in the Numinous,
so clearly shining through them.

All I've Ever Asked

"It's all I've ever asked of you,"
Mystery whispers tenderly in my ear.
"Catch a raindrop on your tongue,
Allow your head to freely nod to music's rhythms,
Do something flirtatious,
Engage in mischief,
Hold nothing back from a good stretch,
Wrap yourself in a quilt,
Savor the complexities of a fine wine,
Listen to, even memorize, a songbird's melody,
Marvel at the cosmos,
Solve an advanced differential equation,
Lend your voice to the minor third
of a mesmerizingly somber chord,
Unreservedly shed a sea of purifying tears,
Let a poem sweep you off your feet,
Notice a breeze's gentle caress,
Slowly run your hand over a textured surface,
Let an ocean wave overpower you, tossing you like a ragdoll,
Behold the 'mightiness' of puppies as they wrestle and tumble,
Laugh 'til it hurts,
Give yourself to silliness,
Be ridiculous,
Then try solemnity on for size,
Explore dignity's many contours,
Drink from the cup of sophistication,
Carefully handle something delicate."

"It's all I've ever asked of you,"
Mystery repeats.
"Awaken to the miracle that is existence.
Take it all in, every last drop.
Majesty is waiting!
She's all dolled-up for you,
reaching for your hand,
standing beside a meticulously prepared
candlelit dinner for two,
a troop of servants at the ready.
Your only job is to look up
from your distractions.
Notice her, give yourself to her.
Give yourself to me."

"It's all I've ever asked of you,"
Mystery chants once more,
this time drawing intimately near,
sealing her lilting verses with a passionate,
unashamedly drawn-out kiss.

Two Questions

Why does the sun
Forever insist
On giving itself away,
Burning and blazing
A billion degrees
No matter what we might pray?

Because that's its nature
It has not a choice
I believe that makes it a slave,
Aren't you glad of the fact
That its chains are intact
Shackled tight to its life-giving ways?

Collusion!

I have a sneaking suspicion
they're all in on it,
every last one.
Conspiring,
feigning ignorance,
acting like it's no big deal.
"How do they play it so cool?"
I often wonder.
How do they come across so nonchalant?
So dégagé?

I do catch them, though,
from time to time,
stealing glances,
snapping their heads back into place,
when I unexpectedly look their way.
Tricky ones, they are!
And well-practiced at their craft!

The operatic brook,
which claims it's merely babbling.
The slow-dancing branch,
who says, "It's just the wind."
The unassuming passerine,
masking the miracle of flight with familiarity.
The flawless voice lilting, "Good night, daddy,"
veiling perfection with a yawn.

You who read this poem,
I suspect you as well.
You're all in on it!
Covering Mystery's tracks,
pretending She isn't animating your every move,
or oozing out your every pore.

"Collusion!" I cry,
in a voice not entirely my own.
Or was it?
Uh oh, could it be I'm in on it too?!?

A Tricky Thing

Capitalization can be a tricky thing.

Laughter, Silence, Matter, Void, Joy, Sorrow,
Love, Stillness, Light, Song, Harmony, Unison,
Energy, Dance, Rest, Tears, Smiles,
Strength, Tenderness, Taste, Sight, Smell,
Touch, Sound, Gravity, Wind,
Disorientation, Conviction, Flexibility,
Faith, Doubt,
Existence.

What word ought not be capitalized,
when God is lurking in them all?

Transcend and Include

We have transcended our religions,
Though we still speak their languages,
And hold them ever dear.

For it was in their narrow confines,
That we first met Mystery,
She Who owns our hearts.

A Flame

I once had so much to say.
I once was so confident, so sure.
I once was the owner of answers so clear,
So definite, so precise.
I once served as certainty's mouthpiece.
I once was truth's own scribe.

But something has changed,
And I now have so very little to say
Or to write.

A flame has descended—
I know not from where—
And rests, white hot, on the tip of my pen,
Not to inspire a flourish of words or phrases,
But to fuse and weld it shut,
That holy silence might reign,
At least for today.

Commissioned

I am a repository of God,
Commissioned,
By Mystery herself,
To be a mischievous little stinker,
To tease,
To poke fun,
To have a foul mouth,
To approach insufferability
By expressing and finding God
In the most unexpected
And inappropriate of places.
What a delightful masquerade She plays,
All dressed up,
As Me.

Abandon Ship

Life is an ocean
Whose ominous depths
Mysterious swells
And unpredictable squalls
Cause us to inordinately cherish
The meager dinghies in which we
Traverse its lengths.

Only a fool, after all,
Would prefer naked exposure to the sea's
Ill-tempered tossings and turnings
Over the sense of safety and stability
So regularly promised and delivered
By the time-worn vessels
To whose railings we cling
With iron-fisted grips
And whose age-old blueprints
Were followed jot-and-tittle
During their patient construction.

But the pensive look in your eye
And the tender tone in which you now speak
Tell me that your skiff's once trusty hull
Has come under critical distress,
Having been dashed against the rocks
With unprecedented violence,
Chilling salt-water now gushing through
Punctures and cracks too many to number,
The familiar methods of patchwork and repair
Only tentatively keeping you afloat
In this precarious moment.

Yes, the situation appears bleak,
But fear not,
For I bring good tidings of great joy:
During the many years, you see,
In which you held festivals in your dinghy's honor,
And while you adeptly patched
Every previously manageable crack in its hull,
I, having long-since jumped overboard,
Was busy crafting a new vessel altogether.

Come aboard, dear one,
Expansive quarters await.
But let's not mince words,
The next step is, by nature, terrifying,
For to get here you must first

Abandon Ship!

Rumi

Give it a try, you say?
Very well.

I once was afloat,
Then I drowned,
Now,
Deep beneath the waves,
Through once dormant gills,
I breathe.

The Miracle

Existence itself.
Existence itself.
Existence itself.

Who needs miracles?
When,
Like a peacock,
The miracle
Struts about
And fans its plumes
Ten trillion times a day.

Today

Let us take two steps forward today
Without taking a single step back.

Let us fall ass-backwards into acceptance today
Without balking at the notion
That it's too good to be true.

Let us unreservedly smile today
In tandem with The Smile
That shines over all,

And is too preoccupied with Joy
To be put-off in the slightest
By our fretful response.

Yes, as for today,
Let us take two steps forward
And not a single step back.

Trust Me on This One

I *yada* for a fact
That God is a She.

You're just gonna have to
Trust me on this one.

These Sacred Words

There is a phrase
I invite you to learn,
A phrase which gladdens
The already glad
Heart of God,

A phrase we somehow
Failed to learn
In seminary,
Sunday school,
Madrasa,
Or synagogue.

Or maybe our souls
Have always known it,
And are simply afraid
To admit they do.

Either way, I know it now,
And I'll gladly fill you in

On the foolproof syllables
That form a glittering key
To unlock the very
Heart of God,
And cause Her, at once,
To take to the streets,
Leading a ruckus parade
Of singing and dancing,
Commanding Her legions
To join in the fray.

These sacred words,
Strung across galaxies,
Perhaps surprisingly,
Number in 6.

So let's clear our throats
And speak them with reverence.
Yes, let us speak them with joy
And delight the Divine.

Ready?
All together now,
On the count of three.

One, two, three:

How the hell should I know?

Another Name

"In the beginning,
God created the heavens
And the earth."

Created? Yes.
But there's so much more
To the story.

For in the time before time,
Mystery stood at the crest
Of a regal staircase.

She, a Tolstoyesque debutante,
Sophisticated, charming, alluring,
Began her descent
Into that primordial ballroom
With a flutter in her heart,

A flutter we now call
The Big Bang.

Then, with a single coquettish glance,
Energy itself was flirted into existence.

And to a batting of her eyelashes,
Space and time responded,
"Yes!"

But flirtation quickly evolved
Into something more,
Setting the tone for all
That was to come.

"In the beginning,
God created the heavens
And the earth."

That's the PG version.

The deeper truth is this:
In the beginning,
God seduced
The formless into form.

And Seduction is but another name
For every moment since.[2]

At a Loss

O, Beloved,

What am I
To do with You?

I keep trying
To have a serious conversation
And You keep
Giving me
That look.

I keep making
Profound points
And You keep
Having something Else
On Your mind.

I keep begging
You to focus
And You keep
Sliding Your hand
Further
Up
My
Thigh.

Two-way Street

Please don't ever forget

That it is a two-way street.

We are hidden with Christ in God,

And

God is hidden with Christ in us.

Deep Beneath the Surface

Just beneath the surface,
yes, we first meet It there,
buzzing,
sparking,
crackling with Energy.

But for those brave souls
who dare hope
for the fullness of God,
a further descent beckons,
through unstable initial currents,
which, if skillfully navigated,
lead to unspeakable fathoms
of luminous darkness,
deep beneath the surface,
where Energy thickens
and Presence congeals
into a blood-red molasses,
before finally succumbing
to a realness so pure,
so dense,
so singular,
It miraculously uncollapses,
releasing a long-held sigh,
as dimensions unfold
and a crystalline mirror takes form
in which the humble
behold their God.

Hostage

Each soul, each creature, each being,
Has taken God hostage
And locked her up inside,
Fretting over a thousand made-up reasons
Why her beauty mustn't be exposed
To the warm light of day.

That's why the universe waits,
Dear one,
With ever-bated breath,
For the revelation
Of the sons and daughters
Of God.

O, that's why God is always wistfully
Looking toward the horizon,
My love,
Hoping you'll one day come into view,
That he might finally find out
What he is.

Too Busy

I'm too busy.

Too busy to not set aside
one day per month for a personal retreat.
Too busy to not be recalibrated
by watching unspeakably wise trees
sway in the gentle summer breeze.
Too busy to not behold water and stones
so joyously fulfill their ancient pledge to gravity.

Too busy to not spend hours in reflection.
Too busy to not pay close attention to my inner life.
Too busy to not slow down
until I spot God hiding in every moment of mundanity.

Perhaps a day will come when I won't be so busy
and these things will become optional.
But for the time being, I have no choice.

I'm simply too busy
Not to reflect
Not to retreat
Not to slow down.

Tsk, Tsk

Others may be
too scandalized to notice,
but I see that mischievous look
in your eye,
Beloved.

We both know full-well
what you've done,
"gifting" us language,
then stepping back,
stark naked,
to have your fun:

We keep trying
to dress you with words,
but they keep sliding off
your shoulders
like so much
frictionless silk,

leaving us nothing
but your infinitely suggestive
Silhouette,
cast against the backdrop
of materiality,
driving us mad.

But that was your point all along,
wasn't it?

Yes, the look in your eye
betrays you!—

All you've ever wanted
is a world full of
tongue-tied,
slack-jawed,
punch-drunk
Lovers.

Tsk, tsk.

You are many things,
Mystery,
but innocent isn't one.

Unexpected Advice

Fear is an unworthy spouse.

That's why the Holy One
Has been whispering
Such unexpected advice
In your ear:

"Have an affair!

Try swimming in the sheets
With Risk and Love!

What better way to make a cuckold
Of that deadbeat husband of yours
Than a three-way!"

Comedy Clubs for Angels

Angels have comedy clubs too,

Their magnificent marquees blinking:

S-E-M-I-N-A-R-Y

Each one a gift to Mystery's spiritual servants,
Brightening their days with uproarious laughter,
As open mics are hungrily seized
By stern-faced, unwitting performers,
Delivering well-rehearsed sets—
Known as *lectures* in the biz—
Much to their undetected audiences' glee.

You should see how they rush from all directions
When their favorites take the stage!

I've watched Gabriel
Frantically craft the text,
"Get over here ASAP!
Trust me, you don't want to miss this."

I've seen Michael
Pee his pants
At the mere mention
Of the word,
"Separation."

I've witnessed entire audiences beg,
"Please stop, our stomachs hurt,
We can't take it,"
Having heard the phrase,
"God is dangerous,"
Repeated but a few times.

But most predictable of all
Is how the heavenly hosts
Spit out their drinks,
Absolutely losing their sacred shit,
Every time they hear the word,
"Two."

Ones and Twos

One is the most sacred word
In any language,
The utterance of which
Makes silence descend
Upon the heavens
And angels bow their heads.

As for two,
No other word
Is nearly
As funny.

The Fate of Saints

Most of us will
Spin in circles,
Arms outstretched,
As we pass through
Those pearly gates.

Then there's the fate of saints
Like Hafiz, Rohr, Rumi, and Barry,
Who clog-up the line
Performing sideways shimmies
As they squeeze their way through.

Heaven just wasn't made
For souls that big.

Calculated Choice

I once was a theologian.

Now I'm a mystic.

Which is to say:

I made the calculated choice
To trade-in being right
For getting laid.

Floodwaters

These floodwaters
Snuck up on us,
Didn't they?

Since we lost track of time
Whispering and giggling about
Love's secret contours.

But that's why the Friend
Gave me to you,
Don't you know?

To remind your soul
Of what it's somehow
Known all along:

That we were always intended
To drown in God,

That Love is a dangerous thing,
Yes, God is a dangerous thing,
For those who'd rather not
Drown.

A Portal to God's Front Porch

God has many desires
But few stronger than this:

To set you free from all your
Correct beliefs
That do little more
Than harass you,

To wrestle from your grasp all your
"This-much-I-know"s,
Snapping you out of the stupor
Of false consolation
By which you've been entranced
For far too long,

To awaken you from your
Rightness-induced slumber,
That you might finally utter
Mystery's favorite words,

"I'm not so sure anymore,"

That fail-safe incantation
That causes God to come rushing
From every corner of existence,

Conjuring a portal,
Before your weary, lovelorn eyes,
To the Beloved's more-than-cozy,
More-than-welcoming
Front porch.[3]

Ill-fitting Saddles

Eagles were never meant
To get around by riding mules.

Yet,
Instead of taking to the skies,
Many keep making adjustments to
Their ill-fitting saddles,

Muttering to themselves,
"One of these days
This'll start feeling right."

Breaking news:
It won't!

Easy A

How else shall we describe God?

She is the ultimate
Moving Target.

For each time we draw close enough
To finally pounce on
Our Divine Prey
She unfairly teleports
Just
Out
Of
Reach.

Cheater.

I swear she stuck her tongue out
At me last time,
Demonstrating her profound eloquence
With the follow-up taunt,
"Na na na boo boo."

Real mature.

But,
She is *also* the ultimate
Easy A.

Nothing, in fact,
Could be easier than God,
And anyone who tells you otherwise
Is lying.

Enough

This.

This world.

Of vibrating strings,
Of quarks, both charmed and strange,
Of orienting protons and neutrons,
Of teasing, dancing electrons,

Of RNA and DNA,
Of bacterium and bacteriophage,
Of fungus and tardigrade,
Of octopus and *Homo sapien*,

Of stone and water,
Of ash and beech,
Of breeze and tempest,
Of sky and sea,

Of good night's sleeps,
Of satisfactions and cravings,
Of indulgence and temperance,
Of Old Fashioned-induced buzzes,

Of asexual heart-to-hearts,
Of forbidden, coy glances,
Of delicate acts of union,
Of tearing each other's clothes off,

Of moons and planets,
Of galaxies and stars,
Of clusters and voids,
Of black holes and quasars.

This.

This world.

Is enough.

For me.

More

How is it, then,
That when it's
Finally
Truly
Enough,
I find out there's
Finally
Truly
More?

Our Suspiciously Prolonged Embrace

This world is a stage,
And God a magician.

The spiritual life is nothing more
Than a series of Divine Prestiges,
With God constantly saying,
"Ha ha, gotcha!"
And me, eyes wide,
Mouth gaping,
Left shaking my head
In Sacred Astonishment.

There are those interludes, though,
During which I always seem to find myself
Rushing the stage
To give our Magician another embrace
And to whisper in her ear,
"Well done, my dear!
Well done!"

And in the midst of
Our suspiciously prolonged embrace,
I perceive,
As though possessing eyes in the back of my head,
(Who's the magician now?)
A satisfied grin spreading across her face.
And with our bodies pressed together as they are
It requires even less effort
To detect,
To feel,
Her grateful sigh.

Spirituality's Most Advanced Activity

Far beyond the realm
Of disciplines and practices
Spirituality's most advanced activity
Is found:

The staring contest.

In which God and the adored
See who can longest maintain
The lover's gaze
Without succumbing to bashfulness
And looking away.

I've won no more than a handful of times,
But you may have spotted
The Beloved and I
Going about our days recently
With big, dumb grins
Plastered on our faces,
Having noticed my triumphs
Have been occurring
With greater frequency.

Somebody Forgot to Tell God

Last night
God had a little too much to drink
And ran around town
Telling everyone
And everything
I love you!

Now the cat's out of the bag!—

And the whole world knows
Just how amorous a mood
The Beloved is always in.

Somebody forgot to tell God
He's not supposed to Drink
That much.

Once Upon a Time

Once upon a time,
The world was safe and good,
And things were plumb-perfect
Between us and God.

Then the monsters came,
Who played to our fears
And told us the great lie:

"There's something off
Between God and you."

O, harm incalculable!

It's a good thing that everything
The Friend has done since
Has been aimed at helping us
Unlearn that lie.

A Thousand Sacred Excisions

Do you have any idea
Just how happy
The Friend is
With you?

Always has been,
Always will be.

Come,
Spend time on my
Operating Table,

And I will perform
A thousand Sacred Excisions
Of all those tumorous lies
That have been planted
In your tender,
Beautiful,
Tormented Mind.

Let my
Golden Instruments
Plunge deep enough
To heal your wounds.

Can't Stop Smiling

I can't stop smiling
Ever since I decided
To take a break from
Humanity's favorite pastime
Of resisting Joy.

I just can't stop smiling
Ever since I made
The brilliant decision
To enroll in an award-winning course
Taught by my two-year-old son.

Sure,
His credentials are questionable,
And he's only got one lecture
Comprised of a single phrase
Put on repeat.

But as it turns out,
It's the only lesson
I've ever needed to learn:

My Daddy happy me.

Now,
Wherever I go,
Whatever I do,
I just can't seem
To stop smiling.

Frozen Bones

I know it hurts sometimes,
Dear one.

Let's be honest: A lot of the time.

I know it's dark sometimes,
Beautiful one—
Yes, I just called *you* beautiful—

But let's be honest: For stretches longer than you'd prefer.

I know you're frightened sometimes,
Precious one.

Being honest: Big chunks of every day.

God, then, must be in on
Some great, cosmic Secret—

For with all the above
Taken into consideration,
She almost never stops asking
Our trembling, solemn species,
The same topsy-turvy,
Unspeakably sacred
Question:

Why so serious?

So come, my love,
Tarry near the warmth
Of my heart's fire,

And let Mystery's Question
Slowly thaw your
Frozen bones.

Pillow Talk

The other night,
Having brushed our teeth
And nestled into the comfort of our
Unnecessarily high thread count sheets,
The Beloved and I
Were playing footsy
And enjoying a little
Pillow Talk.

"I'm so happy about *us*,"
I said,
Oozing satisfaction as I bashfully
Broke our extended eye contact,
Yet continued to run my finger slowly
Along the curve of her arm.
"I love this place we're in."

Placing a finger of her own beneath my chin,
She tilted my head upward
Until our gazes met once more.
"Though many have told you otherwise,
You've always been 'in' with me.
In fact, here's what I want you to do
The next time you have a free moment:

Shout from a rooftop,
Rent a billboard,
Develop a social media campaign,
Write some barely discernable poetry—
Whatever it takes—
To let the world know:
You're in!

For as any sane person can tell you,
The spiritual journey
Is meant to do little more
Than craft in my lovers
The capacity to
Let be what already is."

O, beloved of God,
May you develop the capacity,
Be filled with the grace,

To let be what already is.

Comforting the Comforter

Closing my eyes to pray, I hear some gentle sobbing, as it were, coming from around the corner of the outdoor patio area where I am sitting. I go over there in my mind and find Mystery, in the form of a little girl — vulnerable, emotionally wounded, hurting — sitting on the ground, her back pressed against the wall, head buried in arms crossed atop knees drawn nearly to her chest. She is thin — dainty, but not weak — with hair simply though elegantly arranged in two French braids. Her sobbing isn't particularly loud, but it isn't restrained either. It seems she has been sitting here crying for quite some time.

I sit next to her, my posture mirroring her own, and after a somewhat lengthy silence, I ask, "Are you okay?"

"Yeah, I think so," she gently replies. "It just hurts real bad."

She then turns her head just enough to make eye contact with me before continuing, "It all happens *in me*, you know?"

"Yeah, I know." And another lengthy pause ensues, after which I feel compelled to admit, "It's funny, I've been trained in what to do and what not to do in situations like these, but when the moment comes, my mind often goes blank. Like right now. I'm not quite sure what I should do, so I'm just going to try to not do anything unhelpful. It seems like a safe bet if I were to just sit here with you in silence."

"Thanks. But how about you try one of the things you've learned on me? How about *MAT*?"

"Oh, right: mention, affirm, touch," I expand, gaining a sliver of confidence in the process. "So, yeah, step one: mention. I think you're supposed to put words to what hurts."

"You do it for me, okay?"

"Oh, okay, I can try," I say, nervously drawing in a deep breath at the prospect of trying to describe the inner life of God *to* God. "I think you're hurting because the entire dance of existence takes place in you, all the good stuff *and* all the bad. Every abusive moment, every torturous act, every harmful word: they aren't just things you witness or observe; they are things you feel yourself. You feel them directly, which means you don't have to empathize with us, as though you must imagine what it's like to feel our pain. Our pain happens *in you*. It is *your* pain. And it is A LOT. All of it, every pain of every person — both that of the victim and the perpetrator — is all experienced, felt, and, ultimately, owned by you. Am I putting this even halfway right?"

"Yep, that's pretty much it," she affirms, "and sometimes I wonder if I made the right choice in making myself so vulnerable to it all. But then again, I have this strange feeling that maybe I didn't really have a choice, that this is the only way it ever could've been."

"That sounds really hard. I just feel so bad for you, for all the pain and hurt you feel in every moment. Oh, that reminds me, perhaps now is the time to move to step two: affirm."

"Sure, go for it."

"It makes tons of sense that you'd feel this way," I try to say comfortingly, even as another thought begins to take shape in my mind. "And now that I mention it, it's actually always been your perpetual joy that catches me by surprise. When I see you dancing, it mesmerizes me, but I also wonder how you even do it in the face of human history, filled with irredeemable viciousness as it is. These tears right now, they make sense to me; it's the dancing I've struggled to understand at times."

"Yeah, I could see that. And if I may add my two cents on the theme of things that 'catch you by surprise,' you humans really have been something. I didn't necessarily see you guys coming, and you've taken this whole joy/pain thing to a new level in me. I remember crying before — like when the first supernova ignited, for example — but not like this. I remember being intrigued before — like when the first black hole collapsed in on itself — but not like how you guys intrigue me. I've experienced new depths, new expressions of joy and pain with you in me. You really are something, which is to say, I suppose, *I* really am something."

"Well, again, I just affirm your feelings, your tears. They make a lot of sense."

"Thanks."

"Then there's the 't' of *MAT*: touch. Would it be okay if I put my arm around you?" I ask.

"Absolutely," Mystery says, leaning her head into my chest, as tears trickle down her cheeks onto my shirt.

"I'm so sorry for all the pain that happens in you," I softly repeat.

"Thank you. This has meant a lot to me. It doesn't fix everything; nothing could. But it does help. Thank you for treating me with compassion."

And I squeeze her just a little tighter.

Epilogue: The God of My Experience

Short-on-time,
Irritable,
Questionably bipolar,
Awkwardly transcendent,
Firmly line-drawing,
Stern and somber:
The God I was taught.

Unhurried,
Unoffendable,
Irrepressibly happy,
Astonishingly vulnerable,
Relentlessly erotic,
Playful and shameless:
The God I have experienced.

You?

Acknowledgments

Jo Ann, Heidi, Gary, Jeff, and Russell — the lot of you somehow convinced me that my poetry is worth being put to print. Helping me believe this was no small feat. Thank you.

And three cheers to Drew Tilton and the team at Asio Creative! Your skillful guidance turned this tentative dream into a reality.

Notes

1. The phrase "my sweet, crushed angel" and the concept
    of God as a dance partner that is "notoriously difficult to
    follow" are borrowed from Hafiz's poem *My Sweet, Crushed
    Angel*. See Daniel Ladinsky, *I Heard God Laughing: Poems* of
    Hope and Joy—Renderings of *Hafiz* (New York, NY: Penguin
    Books, 2006), 68.

2. The concept of God "seducing the formless into form"
    comes from *Laughing at the Word Two*. See Daniel Ladinsky,
    The Gift: Poems by Hafiz the Great Sufi Master (New York, NY:
    Penguin Books, 1999), 83.

3. The words "That fail-safe incantation / That causes God
    to come rushing / From every corner of existence" are in-
    spired by *Never Say It Is Not God* found in Daniel Ladinsky,
    The Subject Tonight is Love: 60 Wild and Sweet Poems of *Hafiz*
    (New York, NY: Penguin Books, 2003), 49.